PERSPECTIVE II

WHOSE WHO

Explorations in Christian Identity

PETER L. STEINKE

Concordia Publishing House   **St. Louis   London**

PHOTO CREDITS:

Photos by Bob Combs—5, 14, 50; (Green) 68 and 74
Photos by Waltner—(Black) 20
David W. Corson from A. Devaney, N. Y.—(Green) 20
Photo/Wallowitch—26; (Green) 62 and 80
Greer Cavagnaro—(Black) 74, 84
Photo/Graphics Inc.—(Black) 38
Paul M. Schrock Photos—(Black) 44
H. Armstrong Roberts—(Green) 44
Stephen B. Hyde—56
Berne Greene—(Black) 68
U. S. Army Photograph—(Black) 90
Three Lions Inc.—(Green) 90

Cover: Photograph by Harold M. Lambert

Design by Ed Luhmann

Portions of this book were originally written in study guide form under the same title and published by the Board of Youth Ministry, The Lutheran Church—Missouri Synod. The newer sections broaden the study to include recognition of the psychological and sociological dynamics involved in identity formation. Most of the original parts in the study guide have been extensively expanded. Gratitude is expressed to the following publishers who granted permission to quote from their publications:

Random House, Inc., New York
Harper and Row, Publishers, Inc., New York, Evanston and London
New American Library, New York

Published by
Concordia Publishing House, St. Louis, Missouri
Concordia Publishing House Ltd., London, E. C. 1
Copyright © 1972 by Concordia Publishing House
Library of Congress Catalog Card No. 72-84206
ISBN 0-570-06471-6
MANUFACTURED IN THE UNITED STATES OF AMERICA

whose
way of life
is trustworthiness
and care
shaping all
our children's tomorrows
and mine

We are no longer sure who we are because we do not know whose we are.

(William Lazareth)

WHOSE WHO comes in two sections: WHO outlines some basic ideas about the world outside you, people around you, and feelings inside you. WHOSE illustrates that "you are bought with a price" — you are what you are by the grace of God. It's a Christian perspective of identity, of whose who you are.

Not everyone will be able to agree with what is presented. Perhaps you will find only a few parallels between what you read and what you have experienced. Whether you agree or not, the hope is that you will add your own thoughts and feelings to what you read here. Many of the ideas are stated generally, encompassing a wide range of possibilities. You can enrich them by making it more personal, adding yourself to these thoughts.

Whose? whose? WHOSE? Unless you can attach yourself to something, you will be swept out to the misty seas with no compass or sense of direction, getting lost. You'll suffer the DRIFTS—following pointless arrows, floating feebly in the tide of the latest fad, and feeling unconnected to it all. Without a center (an anchoring point), life's foothold loosens and slips; its foundation weakens all the faster even as you need its support more urgently. When unattached, you drift.

The DRIFTS are sinking, shaky sensations: little makes sense . . . no holds or handles to grip . . . a stubborn fear that whatever appears steady or firm is bending or coming apart. What really fits together or will last for long? And how can you be sure?

Yet youth is a natural time for drifting. Partly because it's the stage of life when searching, questioning, and testing break out of their comfortable caves: What's it all about, anyway? What am I doing? Or why do something at all? But answers don't fall out of the sky. Isn't there something convincing to believe in, and aren't there some people who can be trusted? All you seem to hear are the echoes of your own questions—not persuasive replies.

The DRIFTS are commonly called "identity crises" or crucial moments when you seek the answers to what life is all about. Well, very few young people sit down and sadly ask, "Who am I?" Rather, they *act* it out; shifting from idea to idea, searching here then there, wandering from place to place, creating plans in the morning only to redraw them at night. If you have the DRIFTS, you experiment with different ways of living.

Those who drift, moreover, are not "bad" or worthless or evil or "weird." For youth is also a natural time to shape loyalties, for making connections with significant ideas and people. Drifting is part of that process. Before you can commit yourself to someone or something, you need to know if he or she or it is dependable, trustworthy, and convincing. It is a sign that you value life when you search and search for something or someone to believe in. Understandably therefore, youth regard highly authenticity and genuineness, asking others for truth, honesty, and sincerity. Wanting to make connections, they seek out that which is true and good.

For some youth the DRIFTS are public, that is, obvious and dramatic; among others they are private, hidden and kept quiet, yet known and felt.

But how does one catch the DRIFTS? Perhaps disappointment keeps attacking you: "I'm a failure . . . useless." Or feelings of loneliness stick like glue, "Nobody cares if I exist . . . everybody is against me." Maybe you feel powerless to change anything, and "my actions don't count" lodges in your thought. Possibly a feeling of hopelessness, "it's all cut and dried," drains most of your energies and enthusiasm. Whatever the source, however, either the DRIFTS make you their victim or you make them the growing point for something new, lasting, and meaningful.

While identity development continues as a lifelong process, it is particularly urgent and necessary for young people. For youth is that significant period of life when one wishes to be born again: to awaken to new realities, to become connected with the true and fitting, and to share with others the compelling idea or the significant standpoint.

WHOSE WHO is a look at drifting, finding anchors that can be trusted, and becoming connected with someone and something believable. It's about and for young people whose task at their stage of development is to shape an identity: a *people* to belong to, a *place* to fit into, and a *purpose* to pursue and follow. Likewise it is for adults who might become "believable people" to them.

CONTENTS

WHO

SOME KIND OF LIFE

He who has a why to live for can bear almost any how.

(Viktor Frankl)

SOME KIND OF LIFE

"Pop, I'm a dime a dozen, and so are you." In the play *Death of a Salesman,* Biff honestly reveals how *worthless* he feels. No matter how he added it up, his life was a waste of energy—just another copy of a copy of a copy. "I just can't take hold, Mom, I can't take hold of some kind of life," he complains in another instance. Biff finds himself at a loss—neither at home with himself nor knowing where he is going. No handles. No anchors. No intense feeling of being alive. But Biff's situation offers a clue about developing a sense of identity: "take hold of some kind of life" or you become "a dime a dozen," cut and dried. You don't *stand out* (which is what *exists* means);

rather you drift along as an insignificant dud. And nothing makes sense, nothing takes hold, nothing connects.

Taking "hold of some kind of life" implies being true to something or someone: grasping a few values that make sense, having confidence in people who suggest what is good and true, and investing yourself in some dependable and compelling power. By holding onto *a way of life,* you begin to develop a sense of whom and what you are, becoming a particular person. You live at the *edge* of things, not in a rut. Suddenly and unexpectedly you feel, "This is me, the real me." Without "some kind of life," you have no *standpoint* from which to view yourself and the world. And as is often said, life seems pointless. Answers can't be found for your questions: What am I worth? What can I do that will make a difference? Is there a place for me? How do I wish to live?

But what way of life will give you certainty? Or will anchor you in the middle of the DRIFTS? Why do many ways to center life look good to you at the same time? And are there guarantees that "some kind of life" won't disappoint you in the end?

To find a way of life you experiment, try to fit things on for size . . . testing and testing, again and again losing yourself in the hope of finding yourself. If you're under a hard spell of the DRIFTS, the more uncertain you will be about any way of life. And the more desperate your uncertainty, the more desperate your need to believe in anyone or anything. As your feelings of lostness and unconnectedness strengthen, your desire for a believable way of life magnifies. You become vulnerable to the Answer-Man. Everywhere you turn, you can find "way of life peddlers": Here is the Big Picture! Here is the Super Solution! Here— THE CURE! It comes in the stars (horoscopes), in nature (organic foods), or in activity (candle-making). Or it's obtainable in zen, a suped-up Jesus, drugs, yoga, and money. Perhaps tomorrow it will be available in a bottle containing ink, Ajax cleanser, and pine needles, or in an African dance or in a Robinson Crusoe existence. THE CURE will always promise a "hold on some kind of life"—what it's all about, what you're about—and will endlessly be presented with the sales pitch, "Just believe . . . all you need is faith."

Yet faith is what you don't have, or you hold back. You experience the DRIFTS, wandering because life is empty and dull, without a *point* to it. Regardless of what way of life goes up for sale, it should fill some of the emptiness, sharpen the dullness, and provide a focus. It does this by giving you *people* to belong to, furnishing you with a *place* in life, and a *purpose* to pursue.

A way of life connects you to a person or a group of people. By accepting you as you are, they generate feelings of self-confidence, faith in yourself. You sense that you're at least somewhat significant. Furthermore, they encourage you to direct your newly emerging courage to what some group believes is good and true. In the absence of these good feelings, you wander and roam—perhaps rage in self-hatred. In case after case, people who don't belong, who have not been accepted, end up in the city jail or state mental hospital, in poor housing and in miserable jobs or in broken families and in utter loneliness.

If you receive no acceptance from others, there is no faith in your own worth. And you agonizingly feel out of place. But if a way of life gives you people to belong to, it will provide you with a *place* in the scheme of things. For the acceptance you receive can be turned into self-confidence. You feel like giving or creating something for the world. You feel significant in yourself; you recognize yourself as a part of a whole.

A review of book titles by black writers discloses how black people have been denied a place in life, even an identity: Ralph Ellison's *The Invisible Man;* James Baldwin, *Nobody Knows My Name; The Me Nobody Knows,* a collection of short essays by young ghetto children. Faceless and nameless, they have no place. The way of life in America has kept them "in their place" — out of sight. Blacks become "a dime a dozen"; as the telling phrase goes, "they all look alike." They are not *particular* people or *significant;* they are unable to say I belong *here.*

When you belong to a people and have a place to stand, you are able to move out, reach up, and look forward. Life has a *purpose.* A consistency runs through what you believe about yourself and how others see you. Between what you believe and what you do lies a sense of sameness. You're connected. A lively idea of what life is and ought to be about grows steadily.

Sorting out the believable from the unbelievable is a struggle. Finding people, a place, and purpose promises no easy solution or quick decision. Anyone who makes you believe the opposite, though apparently helpful and certain, offers you a cheap way of life. Self-doubt always remains to play the part of the joker, the mocker of faith; loud scorn . . . the siren that signals your uncertainty; brooding loneliness stands as the footnote to your lack of zeal and enthusiasm. *A convincing way of life is simply one that won't fall to pieces the moment you're threatened by others or your own salty feelings.* It may not have "all the answers," but it is convincing enough to get you through the inconsistencies and unconnectedness, the doubt, the scorn, and the loneliness.

Once again, what way? Before answering, let's explore the dynamics that play a part in shaping "some kind of life."

MOMS & MACHINES

Care is a state in which something does *matter;* care is the opposite of apathy . . . Biologically, if the child were not cared for by its mother, it would scarcely live out the first day. Psychologically, we know . . . that the child withdraws to his bed corner, withers away, never developing but remaining in a stupor, if as an infant he does not receive mothering care.

(Rollo May)

MOMS & MACHINES

A ruler in the Middle Ages tried an odd experiment. He wanted to discover the original language of man. If infants heard no human voices, he thought, what language would they naturally use? The infants spent the early weeks of their lives in the absence of human voices, for the women who cared for the newborn were instructed not to speak in the nursery. Before long all the children died.

Life depends on being recognized. Without attentive care, one lives in a frightening world. Consider the birth and development of a child. She enters as a stranger in a strange world. Helpless. Delicate. Everything is unusual. Chaos. And the continuous crying of the small child—as if she is announcing, "Here I am. Take notice." Indeed those early howls are signals. For the newborn needs warmth, food, stimulation, and touch. But beyond the satisfaction of her physical needs, there is already growing a mysterious need for recognition: to be awakened to hope and life. Thus the importance of the mother's care, assuring her offspring that someone is there and making her feel at home in this new and unfamiliar world. Through the regular and reliable attention of Mom, order comes into the child's confusing, staggering life. The small child is seen, heard, and recognized; she has a "face"—an identity. The mother's care affirms her child, that is, says "yes" to her . . . you're okay—so begins a sense of worth and feelings of being significant.

As time passes, the child combines the caring deeds with the friendly and familiar face of her mother. "This is the face that attends to me." The child who is cared for starts to *trust* the mother who cares. In spite of disorder and strangeness, someone is trustworthy and dependable. This trust deepens, not from *how much* attention the mother gives, but in *what way* she cares. In the mother-child relationship, what matters is the spirit in which the caring is done—the joy, dependability, willingness, and tenderness.

If care gives birth to trust, what happens when the child feels unnoticed, fears her mother does not care? Strangeness widens; chaos intensifies. The child learns not to trust. And intense rage or gloomy withdrawal mark her mistrust. Unrecognized, thereby insignificant and half alive, the youngster may refuse food and smile less. Or maybe she bites and kicks.

Mothers care or don't care, shaping your life either way. With warmth and friendliness the mother encourages in her child a wish to live, to be, and to trust . . . a sense of being special, distinct, and valuable. Even then the road to identity has only begun. For once the child grows, she meets rejection, cruelty, and carelessness. In a short time she can lose courage in herself and turn quite suspicious of everyone else.

Identity begins in being recognized, first by your mother and later by others. No one can live without "face" — being attended to. Imagine yourself in a strange room with unfamiliar people. If they ignore you, you feel odd and peculiar, really strange. "What's wrong with me?" you think. Or, for example, you do something "dumb." "What will others think of me?" Doubt and shame cast their shadow over your insides. Moreover you fear that you are "losing face" — respect and recognition from others. Or someone important in your eyes keeps breaking into your sentences, not allowing you to finish what you have to say. Suddenly you feel neglected and disappointed, as if you're not important to this person. Everyone needs to be needed: listened to, named, faced, and noticed. Otherwise withdrawal or rage emerge, and you're at odds with yourself and suspicious of others.

During the years of adolescence, the need to be recognized takes on a renewed importance, not unlike the infant's need. Youth might be called the time for "a second birth." At this stage of life, however, care and attention is hungered for from a widening circle of people: school friends, teachers, and a special someone from the opposite sex. But it is also the time a new reality dawns on you: Life does not automatically provide you with a caring person, such as a mother during infancy. Besides, life becomes serious business — not very playful. How many times have you been told, "You must become more responsible." You're given a tool and instructed to "make yourself useful." Suddenly time is placed in boxes. You run on a schedule. And machines replace the toys; "produce" is substituted for "go out and play." But you want to be "born again." Where's the recognition? The care?

"Get busy. What did you say? Huh? Recognized? Get to work. Are you a nut or something? Kids . . . too soft these days. Don't want to work . . . want everything given to them. Recognized? Oh, wow . . . too much." Welcome to the Machine World! Move. Grind. Spin. Deal. Whirl. It's wheels, bolts, and buttons; it's paperwork, homework, and busywork. The new reality jumps at you—the Machine runs, it doesn't care. There's the rub. At birth there was Mom caring, and you gradually became a person of worth. But the second birth occurs in the machinery of life. While a mother's care creates feelings of being valuable and significant—accepting you as you are, for what you are—the Machine wants to know what you have done, what you're useful for, and what you have achieved. Then, and only then, will you be recognized.

The Machine: be useful, how can you be used. So some young people *under*achieve, or drop *out;* others curse or attack. What a messy world! Regardless of what action you take, you need a place in life—somewhere that you're cared for, recognized, and given a "face." A person's care can help you feel that you *fit in somewhere.* Like many others living out of place—the poor, the elderly, the blacks, the Indians, the strange—you struggle for a piece of identity, a slice of attention.

No one becomes himself apart from other people. Identity is a gift shaped by someone's care for you, your trust in them. We help create each other.

ON THE MOVE

The search for identity and the search for community are one and the same . . . . To love, men must first find themselves. To find themselves, they must find one another. Identity and community are both found by one same decision: a decision to live in a certain way, a decision to live open to both one's own self and to the self of each of one's brothers.

(Michael Novak)

ON THE MOVE

Movement is magic. To be on the move is to be. Being on the go is being alive. The enthusiasm of youth is rich with the yearning for activation. Sweeping growth (physical, mental, and sexual) during these years propels the golden moments of moving or feeling moved. The time has come for spirited participation: playing around, "raising the devil," and running after something enchanted and curious. In shifting, driving motion, a second birth appears possible and near. The morning dawn is breaking; fresh energy awakens; the new day is here. To stand pat is to betray your youthfulness, to be too old for your age. So — Get with it; hear the language — dig, groove, blast, bomb, turn, and *move!* For feeling moved is feeling you are somebody, as if you're a new man. Anything, just anything — as long as it gives the sensation of moving: a horse or a car, the surf or a ten-speed bike, a pair of skates or skis, even an idea or an event or a person or supernatural powers. These things enable you to feel moved or give you an experience aptly called moving.

Very often this personal need to move or to be moved is best fulfilled and satisfied in a group, now-adays known as a movement. Most youth movements come and go, nevertheless, they are considerably important. Someone has called them "identity work-shops" — places for getting the loose ends together and testing the crusty, hardened limits of business-as-usual. Youth movements arise, though, not simply as channels for blowing off steam or as outlets for excessive energy because of drastic changes in mind and body. In a movement you come upon a way of life: Here is the truth! Your loyalty and trust to it will be strong and committed, for your need of a refresh-ing, stimulating liveliness is being met. Whereas before, life could only be taken as a "drag," now it's afoot in marching strides. Previous days yawned, but now time itself zips. Gone are the DRIFTS — the nagging doubts, the fist full of fears, and the slippery hopes — at least temporarily. After all, life fits together. And you have an inner assuredness that you'll be recognized by those who count in your eyes (*people* to belong to), an experience of being at home with yourself and others (a *place* to be who you are), and a sense of knowing where you're going (a *purpose* to pursue). In the movement is "some kind of life."

Generally, movements are set against the Machine. At your age the Machine has no need for you. You're useless. And the Machine could *care less* or *rec-ognize* little about your need for stirring motion and a new day. Indeed the Machine must drill, grind, and weld. Only a group of youth gathered around a par-ticular way of life, it seems, can offer hope for your need to *fit in life.* When placed outside the one-inch margin or shuttled to the sidelines, your movement is restless. For this reason youth movements develop under certain conditions. What an unjust, rigid, and callous world! You can drift in feelings of *powerlessness, puzzlement,* and personal *pain.* (In the movement you can begin to feel otherwise.)

POWERLESSNESS. If you can't change things, if you're trapped in the claws of the way things are, well, you can despair. Settled in zeroes and negatives, you have no desire to prod and explore the world. Like the unrecognized child, you withdraw to a corner of life, numbed and withering away. Or you can rage. Then come the heated up, fiery words — perhaps a way of insisting upon being heard, seen, and recognized. For youth who feel left out, the way of life is to get right in — to gain a bushel of fairness, a quart of justice, maybe even an ounce of power. The "move" is to gain rule over your own destiny. "Power to the people."

PUZZLEMENT. Stuffy theories. This and that and this and that. Day in, day out. Boxy rules, boxy houses, boxy minds. Can't anyone think in the round? Where are the magicians and the musicians and the mystics? If life is so baffling, so hemmed in and tired out, forget it. For the Machine roars with the deadly howl of STANDARDIZE. You want a sudden, sweet increase of SURPRISE — a moving wonder, an inner flow of oneness, a shared world. But life is split up, cut into halves — one is isolated from two and three can't stand six. "Mind over matter." So Big Thinkers mess up Nature. "Idleness is the devil's workshop." So look busy, you bum. Work is one thing, play another. Moral: all work and no play has made Jack a very dull human being. Among youth who experience life as cut and then dried there's no sense, no meaning to it. Puzzled. Confused. The "move" is to put the pieces in place — perhaps in a commune or in private contemplation or through the all-embracing signs of the stars—to get the pieces of the puzzle together in a pattern.

PAIN. "Do what you want." Yes, do what I want. Who cares? "Can't you see I'm busy." Yes, you're busy, but can't you see I'm lonely. "You'll never amount to anything. Can't you do anything right?" Yes, I can't do much. What's the use?

Uncertain, unwanted, maybe even unusual. You carry with you all kinds of "identity bruises"—wounds of self-hate. Well, try the American Way: liquor, sex, or drugs. Pain-killers. Get out of the I-hate-myself-routine. "Move" outside of your own skin, your own misery, into rapt pleasure, the happy high. Forget the pain in the pulse of the moving group experience.

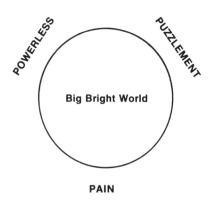

PAIN

The above figure shows three problem areas around which youth movements develop. The circle indicates that youth gathered in some moving, shared experience feel outside the mainstream of life. There is no place for them. No one cares. Nothing is worthwhile. Hopefully, young people believe they can take hold of a way of life through the recognition, care, and trust provided by other members of the group—for "the search for identity and the search for community are one and the same."

HEROES

We should be able to ask every man who desires to lead us that he step forward and show us what his talents have made of him as a whole person. And we should reject the small souls who know only how to be correct, and cleave to the great who know how to be wise.

(Theodore Roszak)

HErOES

Mr. Big. Who is he? Name the beheld, the applauded, the gilded giant—whom we call *hero*. In an opinion poll some adults tried, though the title could not be given to a single person. So the top ten BIGGIES: Oh, forget the names; look what they do. Well, eight are politicians and two are churchmen. Catch on? High value, great worth for *power* and *piety*. Scanning this list, a *New York Times* columnist lamented: no artists or fools, no visionaries or creative geniuses, no risk-takers or oddballs among the ten. Only decency and efficiency are represented. The Solid Man —heads up, elbows in— Mr. No-Drift.

Heroes aren't accidents. They are chosen. In selecting notable politicians and newsworthy churchmen, some adults acknowledged how much they valued control and obedience. For heroes stand for something: a principle, an ideal, an action, or a way of life. If Ralph Nader were chosen, for example, he would represent the value of *fairness.* The "big" guys can't be allowed to rip off the "little" people. Consumer protection, please. Or if Albert Schweitzer made the list, the excellence of *service* would be emphasized. Out in the African sticks. No man's land. Yet here was an intelligent and talented man living compassionately to help the helpless. Mr. Big — someone who has marked the path where before no one else dared or desired to walk, who has stayed at it despite the million and one annoyances of life. He has fulfilled his own possibilities and given you a vision of the good life.

Suddenly the soft hope stiffens — maybe you can make it; who knows? You can be more than you seem to be, greater than what you believe you are. At least somebody has made it. The hero has a "face"; he can face up to what truly counts. Crack up or become unglued? Not Mr. Big — the scheme of things does not overcome him; the pushes and pulls of life cannot make him dizzy. Steady, strong, tested. Just knowing someone has come through it all or keeps at it can freshen your faith in yourself.

A hero — glossy, flashy, nifty. Then, too, the everyday hero, the man or woman who is *special* — a good listener, a "you-can-do-it" supporter, someone who's good for a few laughs, or one who really likes being himself and likes you for being yourself. No fabled leader, popular figure, or front page star — but maybe a neighbor, a teacher, or an acquaintance. When you're in his or her presence, you feel recognized. And you know that you're seen and heard. You're trusted and worth trusting. Perhaps life may be worth trusting?

But what happens if you're desperately uncertain? There *has* to be SOMEONE TO BELIEVE IN. "Speak!

Speak! Tell me what must be rejected, what must be believed. Act! Show me." The hero principle: *Be believable.* Sort out what is convincing, what is not. Slice things down the middle for me—the good and the bad, separate the right and the wrong, the true and the false. I'm back and forth, side to side, and here and there with the DRIFTS. Need Number One— help me put my feet on the *ground* . . . take hold of "some kind of life." Isn't there more than meets the drooping eyes? If nothing is worth believing, what's worth trying?

Remember the child—born in a dazing, befuddling, and staggering world. The earliest need? To look up to someone for food, for affection, for direction. If these needs are not satisfied? Well, the infant withdraws or rages. During youth—the second birth—especially when life is once again perplexing and startling, there is the need for finding someone to "look up to," follow, and believe. For young people, a sense of identity can be as important and necessary as food, handling, and attention is for a child. And identity can't be borrowed or begged. Where are the models for life? The *believable* adults? The waymakers? The hints, suggestions, and clues for being somebody? Or is the choice narrowed to withdrawal and rage?

Strange, but all too true. Where there is driftiness, around the corner there may be rigidness. Under the pressure of the DRIFTS, you can be tempted and pulled into any number of easy answers, slick solutions. Instead of little faith, you plunge wholeheartedly into *total* faith, *complete* devotion to some WAY or WAY-MAKER. Wandering, roaming, undecidedness —suddenly can disappear. Reason: someone reassures you that he has the secret to put your life in gear, in *motion.* Energy flowing aimlessly—now bottled up, tightly packed, squarely boxed. *The* Answer! The future is yours. You *fit* in; you've found your turf, your place. Thus, Hitler and his young troopers; Charles Manson and his "family"; a street gang and its "chieftain." Where once you sought a hero, now you have *over*believed and come up with a boss. But these bosses are interested in the Machine, not you. They want your zeal and enthusiasm, your energies. Interested in *what works,* they couldn't care less, really, about what makes you tick—who you are.

To test the would-be hero: Listen to the tone of his voice. Watch for his readiness to be compassionate. Observe his smiles; watch how he laughs. Is he willing to go out ahead, to show the way? Can he *serve* as well as direct? Will he reconsider his own ideas? See if he is able to forgive. If you could be anyone, is he the one you'd like to be?

One thing is for sure. Mr. Big—whoever he is—cannot make you *believe* in instant identity. If he does, he's offered you a *cheap* identity. He's as phony as a gold nickel. Taking advantage of your driftiness, he simply proposes rigidness. Any way of life that puts forth *stiffness* eventually becomes a *drag.* A little drifting never hurt anyone. In fact, it probably was the condition that led anyone worthy to be called a hero to live as he does or did.

DAD'S WORLD

> The young generation in America is a reminder to us of our finiteness. It directs our attention to the primacy of love over stability. It asks us to consider human relationships more than human accomplishments, a sense of one's own being rather than a sense of success.

(Anthony T. Padovano)

DAD'S WOrLD

The name of the game: Performance. If you achieve something, you are somebody; if you succeed, you are worthwhile. Yes, it's a man's world — where driving, accomplishing, seizing, and dominating are what count. The Big Picture of Dad's world — the achievement principle. Measure a person by his performance! What *use* are you? What have you *done?* How much have you *acquired?* Why isn't your *progress* faster?

Behind any way a person or a whole society lives lie principles — what is believed to be really real, what is true. Around these principles people shape and order their lives. So succeed — that's the aim of life in Dad's world. To succeed you must perform. That's the principle. In achievement rests your personal worth. There's the measure. Who are you? You are what you do—how well and how much.

But many lives are somewhat flat, sour, and at loose ends. Success is far beyond their reach. Still no performance, no recognition. Cling to the Big Picture—achieve a little, at least—and life won't be a complete loss of breath and energy. Keep ahead of the game. So the dime-a-dozen struggle to keep up and keep ahead just to keep face. Immense energy poured out for face-saving: to achieve is to be somebody, to be recognized, to have a face.

Rule Number One . . . Use another's failure as an opportunity for your own success. A sample.

> Boris had trouble reducing "$12/16$" to the lowest terms, and could only get as far as "$6/8$." The teacher asked him quietly if that was as far as he could reduce it. She suggested he "think." Much heaving up and down and waving of hands by the other children . . . She says, "Is there a bigger number than two you can divide into the two parts of the fraction?" After a minute or two, she becomes more urgent, but there is no response from Boris. She then turns to the class and says, "Well, who can tell Boris what the number is?" A forest of hands appear, and the teacher calls Peggy. Peggy says that four may be divided into the numerator and denominator. *(Culture Against Man,* Jules Henry).[1]

Out of Boris' failure rises Peggy's success. At the cost of Boris' misery comes Peggy's joy. Thus many gain a plus identity from someone else's minus identity. Happens everyday—the Jews and the Arabs, the young and the old, the blacks and the whites.

To be sure, it's not a crime to achieve and succeed. But it's only one measure of what you are. Besides, success is a reward in itself. It sparks encouragement

---

[1] Henry, Jules, CULTURE AGAINST MAN (New York: Vintage Books, Random House, Inc., 1965), pp. 295—96.

and self-assurance and confidence. However, the question remains: Can you have a "face" only when another doesn't, like Boris?

Rule Number Two . . . Be right. Exactness, precision, and brass facts. If you're hardheaded and toughminded, your chances of success are greater. Up to a point, that is. Many noted individuals of the past, who now we believe were "right," then were considered "wrong." So be right about the "right things"—the way most people think. But is being right worth the sacrifice of your honesty, if you don't think the way the majority does? If you're always being right to look good—to increase your success—you have a shaky identity. For when you make a mistake, you'll have to spend much time saving face.

The Performance Game—be useful, be right. Dad's world. Very masculine. Win! Conquer! Achieve! But you fail, lose, and mess up—"I'm of no use." Isn't there another *measure* for who I am? Accepting me as I am? Like a mother caring beyond her own self to enrich the infant's life? Giving attention to the *way* I live rather than *how much* I accomplish.

WHAT'S GOING ON OUT THERE

> Our age inspires scant enthusiasm ... ardor is lacking; instead men talk of their growing distance from each other, from their social order, from their work and play ... the drift of our time is away from connection, relation, communion ....

(Kenneth Keniston)

WHAT'S GOING ON OUT THERE

Bombs. White smoke. Fire. The year: 1945. Screaming and crying pierce the air. Stumbling, coughing, choking . . . the place: Hiroshima and Nagasaki. Wild flames. Burnt flesh. Faces scratched by fear. The event: the atomic bombings. Ashes. Odor. "The world is ending."

After the horror of the attack, the scorched land and the twisted bodies became living "memos" of the Bomb. One looked at the dark brown landscape as if it were a dirty oven, wondering if flowers, trees, and grass could ever grow again. Survivors, too, noticed a gradual loss of hair and odd color spots on their bodies. Fever followed after fever. Tormented and shocked, many walked in a trance of death — un-alarmed by the sight of sudden bleeding. After several years, no less, the quick force of wreckage remained, not scribbled or doodled in the minds of the citizens, but deeply carved and thickly imbedded. Death, disease, and dust stalked these cities month after month. Living with both bodily disfigurements and hopeless feelings, those exposed to the Bomb and atomic radiation identified themselves with dying — as if they were tainted and contaminated by it. Overpowered by a massive breakdown of faith in human life, they experienced a loss of the "world." What meaning, after such events, could bring back life to them? The bombings had changed their sense of identity. Now they lived with death sprayed over their insides and with the charred, parched earth around them.

Public events (history) influence your sense of identity. What's going on out there can shape and reshape what's going on inside you. For example, after the second World War, young men returned home marked by the events of combat and military life. Similar to the people of Hiroshima and Nagasaki, warfare had significantly affected their lives. Here is a description of how "what's going on out there" molded the identity of young Americans in the late 40s:

There was also the fact that the war had broken our connections with the past . . . the social structures which had once ordered, contained, and given meaning to our lives — the structures of community, school, parents, relatives, and friends — had all been left behind on the other side of the chasm, and we had a powerful sense of being without identity or place, and an urge that was something near to panic to make structure of home, wife, and children to replace what we had lost. So most of us put aside the brave plans we may once have had . . . and we began to create a culture which was the perfect physical reflection of our impoverished expectations of life. And, not at all surprisingly, it resembled nothing so much as the military world we had just escaped.

From coast to coast we bulldozed the land into rubble, tore out the grass, uprooted the trees . . . the little square boxes of houses set in precise orderly rows could easily have been the married enlisted men's quarters. . . . Families were constantly moving from one housing development to another, like infantry replacements being endlessly transferred from camp to camp. And the atmosphere of military drabness and uniformity lay over everything. (*In the Country of the Young*, John W. Aldridge) [2]

A generation stung by war weariness — in Hiroshima and Nagasaki, *death,* and in the United States, *drabness* — struggled to make sense out of life, to discover who or what they would become. The moods and events of the times touched and changed the kind of life they lived.

What's going on out there? What are the events that might influence you? At school? In the home? In any problem or situation puncturing your life.

[2] Aldridge, John W., IN THE COUNTRY OF THE YOUNG (New York, Evanston, and London: Perennial Library, Harper & Row, Publishers, 1969), pp. 4—5.

WHAT GOES DOWN COMES UP

> "We are all seething with contradictions; it is only with difficulty that we admit the fact to ourselves, and we take great care to hide it from others."

(Paul Tournier)

WHAT GOES DOWN COMES UP

"You can't keep a good man down." So thought your grandparents and great-grandparents. With get up and go, grit, and nose to the grindstone, a man could make himself a success, find a "place" for himself. Hard work. Stick-to-it-ness. Up, up, and up. What a wonder: from the backwoods to the front page, from obscurity to prominence. "The cream always rises to the top," the small town wisdom had it.

At the same time, however, a few of the grandparents' contemporaries were saying, "You can't keep a *bad* thing down." By that they intended to say — keep the lid on anything disturbing and ugly. Ban the unwanted difficulties. Yet they returned; they

were remembered. No matter what was pushed down, sooner or later it would come up again. Hold back your lion-like anger; keep down the fear; squeeze tight your itchy doubts. Suddenly—"Pop!" What goes down comes up.

Action and reaction. Force and counterforce. Press down and pop up. And conflict. "Keep out of sight," for example, the people who are of "little use" to the Machine: herd into housing off the beaten path (ghettoes), stuff into isolated areas (Indian reservations), and make the useless less visible (institutions for the mentally retarded, the emotionally disturbed, and the elderly). But whammo! The unseen demand to be seen—the unheard to be heard. Or put down feelings in the name of reason. Emotions mess up the Machine. But young people come along and ask, "What's wrong with what you feel?" What Dad's world suppresses, youth want to resurrect. They take Dad's second-rated values and make them first rate. Another example: Dad's world elevates Father Progress and abuses Mother Nature. But some youth turn the tables, insisting that the "good earth" is more important than the "great machine."

Individually, each of us *hides* the disgusting and embarrassing things about ourselves. Put down what you don't want to come up. Strategies: hide your uncertainties under the lid of overconfidence . . . exhibit a calm optimism while behind the scenes a rowdy despair kicks its heels. Engaging in "put-downs" and "out-of-sights" creates *pressure,* like steam under a pot's cover. *Repress*—control, restrain; *suppress*—defeat, bottle up; *depress*—flatten, lower; *oppress*—annoy, crush. If the tension underneath grows strong, the lid will blow off. Things go to pieces.

To be somebody, however, means to be *all* you are —the pluses and minuses, the successes and the failures, what you keep up and what you keep down. What *kind of life* enables you to accept it all? To have the courage *to be?* To become somebody despite the evidence you might be nothing?

WHOSE

SUPEr i / POOr ME

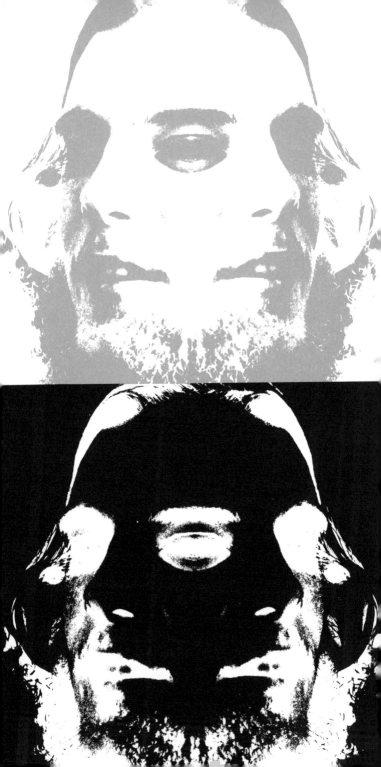

"What happened to the crow, Zorba?"

"Well, you see, he used to walk respectably, properly — well, like a crow. But one day he got it into his head to try and strut about like a pigeon. And from that time on the poor fellow couldn't for the life of him recall his own way of walking. He was all mixed up; don't you see he just hobbled about."

(Nikos Kazantzakis)

SUPEr i / POor mE

Sticky days, hard times. All at once — a swirling life. Nothing holds together; things fall apart. DRIFTS in-here; DRIFTS out-there. Nothing, nothing is firm, solid, or fastened. Unattached. A stranger. A misfit. A dwarf. As one young person put it:

> I feel like a three-wheeler on a busy expressway. I'm out of place, just "out of it." Where do I belong? Sometimes I feel like a fish swimming but someone comes along and tells me I should be a bird flying, or an ant toddling. Trying to be myself . . . then some "nut" keeps telling me: "make something of yourself" and "grow up." How can I? How can I grow unless I start

with myself, what I am, from my own roots? Is life a lead pencil—its point always broken when pressed down too hard?

At a loss. Where is the point to life? Why don't people help you *sharpen* it, rather than pressing down on it, breaking it? Crushed. Restless. Things go to pieces. No stable direction. Wanted—*some kind of life.*

Without an anchor—the DRIFTS. If life is pointless—well, friendships can be short-lived, ideas can shift overnight, and "high" at breakfast may only be "low" by suppertime. You wait for some event or some person to sweep you out of the DRIFTS with the promise of a point to it all.

Meanwhile you have to handle this confusion. Two methods: the "proof" and the "pity." The proof method involves pretending to be *more* than you are. If you feel inwardly unsure, you attempt to make up for the inner deficit by outer performance. You over-act, overstate, and overpledge. No one else seems to care about you—so you try to *prove* that you are *somebody.* Cocky. Dead certain. Being "It." Thus the *Super I.* On the other hand, the pity method plays with being *less* than you are. You feel uncertain, and you let it be known. *Poor Me.* Through someone's pity, you're looking for some kind of recognition, some care. By being a loser, you hope for some *approval,* some confirmation of how hard you've had it. If you can't be known and recognized for what you've *done,* at least some one might notice your misery, take pity, and "see" you. Look what the world has done to me! Immense sadness. Moodiness. Acting like a nobody, yet wanting to be treated as somebody.

Prove yourself: The Super I. Be approved by others. The Poor Me. Either way you search for cheap care. The proof method fails because you need to be cared for, to be recognized. But you're in no position to receive it; you're too busy trying to do it for yourself. If you refuse to accept what you are, you hardly want others to accept you as you are. The fallacy: Someone else's care creates "somebodyness," not your own cheap care. Your care for yourself, in this case, is a way to keep down and out of sight your own self-hatred. And the pity method works no more effectively. You *contrive* the situation. What others will not give you naturally and spontaneously, you scheme to get by playing the role of the picked on, the to-be-pitied. Actually you try to *force* or to manipulate someone into caring for you. But approval by pity is cheap, too. For if you believe you can be recognized only by being a nobody, you'll never leave the role. You'll always be the victim. By circumstance you're committed to hating yourself. It provokes attention.

Put a stop to your aimless wandering. Quiet the inner, noisy doubts. Use the proof or pity methods: live *above* or *below* what you are. Still, you're not able to accept yourself *just* as you are. To be somebody—do you have to pretend?

How comical, how tragic! Jules Feiffer captures this in a cartoon. A boy named Danny says,

Ever since I was a little kid I didn't want to be me. I wanted to be Billie Widdledon. And Billie didn't even like me . . . I walked like he walked. I talked like he talked. I signed up for the same high school he signed up for . . . Which was when Billie Widdledon changed. He began to hang around Herby Vandeman. He walked like Herby Vandeman. He talked like Herby Vandeman . . . And then it dawned on me that Herby Vandeman walked and talked like Joey Haverlin and Joey Haverlin walked and talked like Corky Sabinson . . . So here I am walking and talking like Billie Widdledon's imitation of Herby Vandeman's version of Joey Haverlin trying to walk and talk like Corky Sabinson. And who do you think Corky Sabinson is always walking and talking like? . . . Of all people—dopey Kenny Wellington. That little pest who walks and talks like me.[3]

[3] Feiffer, Jules, HOLD ME (New York: Signet Book, New American Library, 1964), pp. 92—95.

Danny, too busy trying to be what he is not, makes no effort to be himself.

You don't have to pretend to be *more* or *less* than you are. That's the message of the Good News — God accepts you *as* you are. He cares for you; He recognizes and accepts you. You no longer have to stand before God with your achievements in hand. Nor are you permitted to try. Indeed nothing you perform enables God to accept you — whether you perform the role of Super I or the role of Poor Me. God's care and recognition is given, not *because of* what you are, but *in spite of it*. He acts through His Son, Jesus Christ, to reconcile you to Himself. In the life, death, and resurrection of Jesus Christ, you see the gracious face of God, the God who is for you.

True, God puts you *under the pressure* of His judgment. And you want to blow the lid off — arguing, questioning, and quarreling with Him. But He wants you to see yourself as you are. As someone said, "In a dark time the eyes can see." There — in the darkness — you see the pains, sins, and hurts. You know what you are. But it is precisely there that God cares. What He puts down, He lifts up.

God's forgiving care accepts you *as* you are. It's the in-spite-of method. No further need to pretend. Now it's time to accept His acceptance. "To those that believe on His name He gives power to become the sons of God." His CARE enables you to TRUST Him and yourself and the world. For if you are ready to live out of God's gift of life, you can accept yourself as somebody — always loved and always recognized. God's *believable;* He gives both the *care* you need to have a "face" (an identity) and the faith to *trust* Him, to have a place in life. Just as He accepts you in spite of yourself, you can also accept all of life in spite of the loose ends and sticky days. Life has a center and a direction despite the DRIFTS. Though you are faithless, He is faithful. For He cannot deny Himself.

MiNi-rESURRECTiON

. . . unless a grain of wheat falls into the earth and dies, it remains alone; but if it dies, it bears much fruit.

(John 12:24)

MiNi-rESURRECTiON

God never promised you a rose garden. Weeds and dust, wind and drought—life hardly comes out smelling like fresh flowers. But neither did God promise only crabgrass and a sandy lawn. Life is a mixture: good and evil shaken together, weeds and roses growing side by side, being at home and being in the wilderness. What God promises is a *way out* of the weeds—a few roses to boot.

Now some would make you believe that life can be split down the middle. They draw a yellow line through life, separating the good guys from the bad guys. Here the weeds; there the roses. They falsely portray the Christian way of life as all roses. Thus, stay your distance from the bad guys; keep out of the weeds of the world; mind your own (religious) business. From what was said before, you can detect what they're up to—trying to gain a *plus* identity from someone else's *minus* identity.

Likewise they deny their God-given identity. Actually they are rejecting God's care and acceptance. He did not intend that the forgiven stay their distance and put weedy characters in their place. To be cared for is to begin to care for others—to reach out, to be gracious, and to drop the *negative labels* placed on any man. Martin Luther wrote:

> When God commands me to love the neighbor, He excludes nobody, neither friend nor foe, good nor evil. For even if a man is evil and does evil to you he does not lose the name "neighbor." He remains your flesh and blood and belongs in the commandment, "Love thy neighbor."

All attempts to put down another denies him a "face." But your identity does not depend on labeling others as inferior, evil, or bad guys. It is through God's care that you have a "face," not by denying one to another person. If you are unsure of God's care, you attempt to save face. The inner, ugly weeds—keep them out of sight. To accomplish this, keep looking at the evil in another.

Yet God never demanded: "Deny evil." Even though He knows what is in man, including the evil, He cares. For instance, you are given a "face" in Baptism. God *identified* you: recognized, loved, and forgave you. Before you could ever prove yourself or try to gain God's approval, He cared. Evil isn't denied; it is there. And it is overcome. Thus, life doesn't fall to pieces.

What was begun in Baptism continues—you die to sin and come alive to God. Dying and rising: the Christian *way of life.* Again and again and again, the Super I or the Poor Me is put to death, and a New Man arises. The church calls it the confession and the absolution, the laying bare of personal evil and the announcing of the good news of God's care for you . . . NEVERTHELESS. For this reason Christian worship is an "identity workshop," where you come to know *whose who* you are . . . when you can bloom from where you are planted — in the mini-resurrection of "you are forgiven."

The New Man: What is he like? Successful? Perhaps, perhaps not. But the achievement principle no longer counts. So the New Man need not be successful. Nor is he perfect. As Martin Luther said, "One and the same man is . . . righteous and sinful, good and evil." The New Man is compassionate. He is "most active among the poor, the needy, the evildoers, the sinners, the insane, the sick, and the enemies" (Martin Luther). He seeks out those who are faceless, who think life is pointless, who have no place to be somebody. He who is cared for is somebody — has a "face." The need to gain an identity by degrading another is useless. He can face up to the needy, refusing to *label* them the bad guys. For he knows what he does or leaves undone "for the neighbor is done or left undone for God Himself." God never promised him a rose garden but agreed to meet him in the weeds of the world. And if he serves ("dies to himself"), he "brings forth much fruit."

TALE OF TWO SONS

Is it really possible to speak of brothers where there is no father, and who can assume the role of Father of all men save the Creator of all? If you truly want to be the brother of all men you have to accept your role as son, you have to receive and live the life of God — and the more fully you are a son, the more fully you will be a brother. . . . There are some who think it suffices to become one with God without bothering about their brothers. If you really want to be a son of the Father, you have to accept your role as a brother of all his other sons. When you reject a brother, you reject the Father as well, you are in fact denying the Father.

(Michael Quoist)

TALE OF TWO SONS

The younger son: "Father, give me the share of property that falls to me." The blood was running fast in his veins. "Ah, to taste life — finally." A little excitement. A few moving experiences. He had to get away. Taking "all he had," he travelled "into a far country." Now — going places and doing things. Wild!

But he wasted everything "in loose living" — the DRIFTS? To make matters worse, he couldn't find a job, his friends left him, and he had no choice but to stick around town. He did get a job, however, feeding pigs — the shame of it, for a Jew. What a drag and disgrace.

He left for home, willing to become a servant to his

father—if only he could eat well. "I'll just have to confess that I'm not worthy to be called his son." Approaching town, he was met by an excited and welcoming father: "This my son was dead, and is alive again; he was lost, and is found."

Music, dancing, singing, and laughter broke through the doors and windows of the home that night. Party time—the coals were smoking and the steaks broiling. Soon the elder son appeared at the back door. "What's all the noise about?" When he learned that his brother had returned, "he was angry and refused to go in." Brooding, cursing. He felt hurt. But his father invited him to join the party. Bursting with rage, the older son shouted: "I never disobeyed you. All this time I served you. Now this son of yours who made a fool of himself comes home and you have a big celebration. Meanwhile I'm left in the fields slaving with my hands—no one thought about calling me. Besides, why didn't you ever give me a little goat —just a little goat—for a party with my friends. This good-for-nothing son of yours hasn't accomplished a thing . . . not one thing. Oh, but he gets a fat calf. It isn't fair! Forget it! Have your lousy party!"

His father reminds him: "All I have is yours." As the older son sulks and walks away, the father says, "It is fitting to celebrate—your lost brother has been found."

Where is justice and fairplay? Surely the elder son has a case: loyal to his father, a hard worker, dependable, and always obedient. But the do-nothing younger brother receives the father's attention and recognition.

Here two principles come into conflict—the achievement principle and the in-spite-of principle. Which of the two should measure the situation? Obviously, the father and the elder son see things differently because each measures according to opposite principles.

The situation: The father cares for his youngest. He recognizes this son despite his past behavior. To his elder son's charge of unfairness, the father replies, "All I have is yours." He too is cared for and recognized. The father is not playing sides. On the contrary—he is accepting each son as he is. The father loves the eldest not for what he has accomplished, just as he loves his youngest even though he accomplished very little. The older son thought if he wasn't measured by his performance, then what good is he? He wants his father's recognition to be based on what he's done, especially in comparison to the younger brother.

But the father refuses to play by the rules of distribution: so much done, so much given. His care isn't a bargain; it's a gift. For instance, the father extends his care both to the youngest who left home in *puzzlement* and to the older son who felt *powerless* in the seeming injustice of the father. Both remain sons, nevertheless. In neither case would the father *label* his sons or *reject* them. The Big Picture in the father's world: acceptance in-spite-of the sons' behaviors.

The elder son demonstrates, though, an identity crisis. He didn't know whose who he was. Believing that his father's acceptance of the younger brother was a repudiation of himself, he walks away crushed and upset. What he would have to discover is that the father accepts his sons for what they are. His identity depends not on his own achievement, nor on the minus identity of his brother, but on the basis of the father's care—despite all the efforts of the son to make himself more acceptable, both to his father and to himself.

To be sure, when you doubt your identity—your place and purpose in life—you often lose your brother in the process. Notice the elder son's sharp remark to his father: "this son of yours"—as if the youngest were not *his brother.* A weak identity leads to the belief that the other is always a competitor; a strong identity recognizes another as a possible *companion.* Companions are not at each other's throat but at *play* together. Play and companionship cannot be divided. True companions play together, celebrate their shared delights, and enrich the joys of being somebody to oneself and to another. For the struggle to be somebody becomes the struggle to live with others.

God measures you. His Big Principle: the death and resurrection of Jesus Christ. Whatever is lost can be found; the dead made alive; the wrongfully committed in the past, forgiven; hidden in proof and pity, laid open, recognized, and changed.

EUCHARISTIC ENERGY

> No one knows how it hurts a young man to avoid happiness and to cultivate solitude and melancholy . . . I, who have hitherto spent my life in mourning and sadness, now seek and accept joy whenever I can find it.

(Martin Luther)

EUCHARISTIC ENERGY

If you know whose who you are, your life can bounce and bubble. Indeed, the Christian's life is ever marked by some bouncing and bubbling. Perhaps it's difficult to rid yourself of the idea that the Christian way of life is somber, glum, and sober. Yet the early Christians were not known for being sour and severe. Their enemies never charged them for being sad and dreary. They knew the mocking and stinging of life, but these Christians didn't spray the world with lemon juice or wave a mean stick. Their way of life too grim? No — too joyous to be true. And at the center of it was a shared meal, called Eucharist — joyous thanksgiving. Why not? After all, life made sense to them. Uprooted, strangers—but believing God cared. Hunted and hounded, yet confident in the promises of God. So when they gathered together —the joy and thankfulness of it all. They were *moved* by the Spirit of God; they *moved* generously toward one another. The early Christians had found a way of life that wouldn't go to pieces. Confident in the certainty of the Resurrection, they radiated hope to everyone who needed it, and everybody needed it.

Life was worthwhile—"okay." It was a gift, given through a God who cared. The *way* they chose to live, then, was filled with eucharistic energy—a response of thanksgiving and rejoicing. This energy enabled them to be "long" on generosity: nothing is totally uncheerful, nobody completely insignificant or without possibility. In giving care to the needy, they said, "Thank you." Grateful to God's gift of acceptance in Christ, they set about to care for the nobodies around them. No wonder these early Christians gathered around the meal their Lord commanded and called themselves the "offerers." For they had received the mercies of God and in return were ready to offer themselves in faith to Him and in service to others. And the *spirit* of it all: a joyful and thankful way of life.

God has a unique genius for caring. The name of the game: Resurrection. Whatever has grown cold, stale, and old can be created fresh and alive. Man is redeemed by Jesus—born again. He has a "face." And once more he becomes a child. Like the child, he *plays.* New zest. An upsurge. Sparkling enthusiasm. The root meaning of enthusiasm means *to be grasped by a god.* Thus, the first followers of Christ—grasped by His care and noted for their eucharistic energy—bubbled over and bounced around in the hope of finding new companions. Resurrection play: losing yourself and finding yourself in care for others.

But if you are convinced that you are a nobody, you'll feel that you have nothing worth *offering.* If you're certain that nothing fits together, once again you'll feel hopeless, at a distance from others. Down the drain goes courage. Resurrection play never turns into motion. You're bogged down in self-hatred, self-despising, and self-mistrust. When life gets stuck and gets the best of you, very little is left to do. Like a kite trapped in a tree, your source of energy is gone. Gladness and generosity slip away.

The Eucharist: an occasion for receiving new courage to be yourself. To be forgiven is to start again. *Failure is disposable.* And starting over again is always like a game—a playful time, high energy, and good friends.

BEING DIFFERENT

. . . Jesus, well aware . . . that He had come from God and was going back to God, rose from table, laid aside His garments, and taking a towel, tied it round Him . . . and began to wash His disciples' feet and to wipe them with the towel.

(John 13:3-5 NEB)

BEiNG DiFFErENT

An old maxim: "When in Rome, do as the Romans do." When the apostle Paul wrote to the Christian people of Rome, however, he urged them to do exactly the opposite. "You people in Rome, don't do as the Romans do." For what reason? By the *mercies of God,* be different. You are called by the Gospel to be set aside for God's purposes, to be unique and significant. "Away with the monkey-see, monkey-do business," Paul suggests. "You can't go into life playing follow the leader, or repeating, 'me too, me too.'" Whose who are you? Are you trapped in the whims and wishes of the world? Or are you by God's mercy *His who.*

For sure this means you cannot conform to the Big Picture—the achievement principle. It neither measures you accurately nor anyone else. Paul's words challenge you to give up this single-minded and flat view of life. Often those who are judged *worthless* are condemned under the law which says that unless you succeed, you are nothing. But the *mercy of God* doesn't measure you by success or usefulness but announces that *anyone can be saved.* Refuse to label people with the intent of checking them off according to the Big Picture.

To be Christ's person doesn't mean you stop being a Roman but you become a different kind of Roman. Just as you know that you are many things, likewise you understand that everyone is. The big difference in the Christian way of life: you know that a person can be a new man, can be more than he presently is, that many possibilities exist. What might the useless become? How much more might happen if you encouraged the weak or crossed over to be with the hopeless? To be different means to look at another as a fellow human being, not to be indifferent to him, to avoid him, to put him away, or to label him.

If you know *whose who* you are, the need to be somebody at the cost of another's dignity dies off. Instead you *recognize* the other and care for him.

The achievement principle concerns the calculative; weighing, totaling up sums, adding, and subtracting. It's distributive—to each as he has performed according to the *world's* standards. To be in Christ—to be different—means you have a new measure; it's *creative.* How can I *care* for another and *encourage* him to become somebody?

Finding yourself includes finding your neighbor. What's going on out there leads you to believe that it's each man for himself. Elbow and shove; get a place for yourself. But *be different.* You are known by God, cared for, and recognized. Thus, be looking for the other—especially for the reject. There's a place for both of you—by the mercies of God.

i COUNT, YOU COUNT

If you believe in the kingdom where every-thing might become a miracle, where all men might become new creatures in God . . . and you are willing to suffer that it might be so, then you believe in God.

(Samuel Miller)

i COUNT,
YOU COUNT

To be somebody. But you've realized that it's no easy task. On the one hand you may believe you're too good, on the other hand you're not much. The score-board reads:

> Super I—"I count; you don't."
> Poor Me—"You count; I don't."

But no one counts if both don't. Each person must make a difference to the other person. What happens to personal relationships when one counts for something but the other one is discounted?

The discounted: an *it*, a *thing.* He'll be viewed as *soil* where another can plant his own ideas; as a *devil*, someone to be cursed and exposed; an *animal* to be tamed and driven; a *machine* to be greased and run.

Perhaps you've felt discounted. You've been labeled a good-for-nothing, a long-hair jerk, a screwball, or a phony. But like anyone who's been discounted by prejudgment of his identity or over-labeling, you scorn and deny the tags you have been given. You need to say what you're not, to deny what doesn't fit you . . . shouting it, tearing off the lousy labels glued on you—as if you were a tin can or an envelope. Unfortunately some of you may simply accept your lesser value, your discounted price. And you become exactly what careless people expect you to become. Why fight? It's easier to be nothing at all. You'd rather drift, mistrusting your own ideas about yourself, disbelieving that it's possible for you to do something of value.

In the *Christian way of life,* you count. Even though you are called a sinner, you are also called a son of God. God has no interest in labeling you, giving you a minus identity. So one of the Lord's apostles exclaims: "See what love the Father has that we should be called the sons of God." And sons we are indeed.

And if you count, what about the other? If you trust that God cares for you, isn't that enough? Can't another take care of himself? After all, faith is what *counts.* God knows, you have sufficient trouble just trusting Him, no less troubling yourself about someone else? But what is given to you—an identity—is not a *private keepsake.* God identifies you through His care; He *sets you aside for a purpose:* to care for your neighbor as you care for yourself, as you have been cared for in Christ.

Luther once set up this example: If Jesus Himself or His mother were sick here and now, everyone would gladly help. "Everybody would have daring and courage and nobody would flee, but people would volunteer help." Then he adds, "All this means that we do not hear what Christ Himself has said, what ye have done to the least, that ye have done to Me. . . . Here you can hear it yourself that the love to the neighbor is as important as the First Commandment, the love of God. And what you do or leave undone for the neighbor is done or left undone for God Himself."

By God's grace, you count. When you face any needy person, He says, "Remember, he counts too." So Jesus, knowing whose who He was ("had come from God and was going back to God"), took a towel. He knew he counted, and with a towel He recognized His disciples — they counted too.

THE MAKING
OF A CAFE CULTURE

For the love of Christ controls us, because we are convinced that one has died for all . . . that those who live might live no longer for themselves but for Him who for their sake died and was raised. From now on, therefore, we regard no one from a human point of view . . . if any one is in Christ, he is a new creation . . . . God, who through Christ reconciled us to Himself and gave us the ministry of reconciliation . . . entrusting to us the message of reconciliation . . . . God making His appeal through us.

(2 Corinthians 5:14-20 RSV)

THE MAKING
OF A CARE CULTURE

Spinning and spinning — who can stand still? A puzzle with missing pieces — who can lie down and rest? Turn over the rug; peek under the couch; check your pockets. What kind of a life is this? How strange? There is. There isn't. Isn't there? What is there? Is there — SOME KIND OF LIFE?

"A Christian kind of life — is it a kind that makes sense, holds things together, or inspires? Can it pry open the locked meaning of it all?" "What do I care to make of myself : And what do I have to work with?" Just what does it have to say about that? Can it supply the missing pieces?

Well, here it is — simply at least. The Christian "kind

of life" begins with "you are not your own, you are bought with a price." Whatever you are, you are by God's grace. Confused, stunned, and lost . . . like a newborn child. But there is One who cares. You are recognized—a "new face." That's *new creation*.

God identifies you. You are His. In caring for you, He creates and stirs up a sense of trust. Enabled to trust Him, you can begin to trust yourself, another, and life itself. And trust spreads out. It cares in turn, putting you "on the move." Ready to do something and go somewhere; but what and where? Here are a few answers from a young man, who suffered the DRIFTS but was grasped by grace:

> Then it (care) goes out lavishly and open to everyone who needs it, and meets both good and bad, friend and foe.

> . . . you offer yourself to your neighbor and serve him, wherever he needs you and every way you can, be it with alms, prayer, work, fasting, counsel, comfort, instruction, admonition, punishment, apologizing, clothing, food, and lastly with suffering and dying for him.

> All works of love, then, must be directed to our wretched needy neighbors. In these lowly ones we are to find and love God, in them we are to serve and honor Him, and only so can we do it.

> Go and take the money with which you were about to build a church and give it to thy neighbor. Look to your neighbor how you may serve him. It is not a matter of moment to God if you never build Him a church, as long as you are of service to your neighbor.

> So God would much rather be deprived of His service than of the service you owe your neighbor, and would sooner see you less stringent in your service toward Himself, if you are pious at the expense of serving your neighbor.

> For we must serve the world and do good unto it, even if it repays good with evil.

... those slippery, flitting spirits that seek after God only in great and glorious undertakings .... But they miss Him by passing by Him in their earthly neighbor, in whom God would be loved and honored.

This love does not consider its own reward or its own good but rewards and does good .... This keeps love busy, always and everywhere. And note how this commandment makes us equal before God and suspends all differences of calling, person, rank, and work.

What "nut" said those things? A young man who wanted "to take hold of some kind of life," who had the DRIFTS, and who had agonized under the achievement principle. Martin Luther, no less.

But you have to be a nut, in some sense, to be a Christian. An apostle of Christ spoke of being "fools for Christ." In many cultures the fool has been traditionally the "misfit," insignificant in the Big Picture, a nonsuccess according to the Big Principle: dwarfs, the physically deformed, simpletons, the poor, and the inferior. And today our culture, like the past, takes its fools from the little people or little things in the world's eyes . . . Charlie Brown, a child . . . Snoopy, a dog . . . Hazel, a housemaid . . . Brother Sebastian, a monk . . . Mickey Mouse, Bugs Bunny . . . Tonto, Jughead, Amos and Andy, Blondie, Little Orphan Annie . . . .

It takes a fool to serve — to be little in the Machine . . . to do good even if good is repaid with evil . . . not to "consider (one's) own reward" . . . to "suspend all differences." . . . For the Christian way of life includes both trusting in a God who cares for you and caring about needy people in serving them. To the question, "Whose who are you?" the Christian response is that I am God's by grace through faith and my neighbor's through care. That's identity! And it's foolish.

If you are God's and your neighbor's, you begin to put the pieces of the puzzle together. Instead of spinning and spinning, you set out to make a new world, a care culture: serving *people,* making a *place* for them, and acting out the appeal God makes through you, that is, having a *purpose.*

Making a care culture is *some kind of life.* You *delight in* and *suffer for* another. Indeed somebody *matters* to you, makes a difference. You're willing to stand by, having been *there* yourself where now someone else suffers the DRIFTS. And your care is a way of thanking God for what you have received — an identity. You thank by caring, offering more understanding and less nasty labelings. For care without the *spirit* of joy is duty, performance — the achievement principle. Furthermore it's a *top-heavy* care — "over-protection" — making the other dependent on you. But true care *seduces,* drawing the other out of himself and helping him recognize his own worthiness. Care rejoices; it's the celebration of one who knows whose who he is.

You begin caring for *particular* persons, not the whole needy world. Care moves little by little. For William Blake warns, "he would do good to others must do it in Minute Particulars; General Good is the plea of the Hypocrite and Scoundrel."

From what is near and specific, care moves out to confront the wider issues. It is as useful a service to care for a person that he might avoid his problems as it is to care for him after he has a problem. "For it is . . . as good as giving alms, if one helps a person so that he does not need to become a beggar, rather than to give alms and help those that have become beggars," says Luther. Someone else has challenged, "Suppose for a minute that hundreds of Good Samaritans saw a thousand battered men lying on the Jericho road. Would they begin to make a care culture by simply piling the victims on asses and taking them to a social or health agency? If the Samaritans did not have sense enough to ask what ought to be done to make the road between Jerusalem and Jericho safe for pedestrians, the asses would begin to inquire into the causes of their overwork." The making of a care culture includes both helping the disturbed person and changing the disturbing situation.

If God is for you, and He is, isn't it true that He is for everything created? Thus, Christian worship—the identity workshop—concludes with "The Lord . . . make His *face* to shine upon you and be gracious unto you," preparing you for the *purpose* of facing needy *people* and sharing with them the *place* where all men fit—the grace of God.

Suggestions for Study

If you use this book in groups or for study, you might find it helpful to match the sections in WHO with those in the second part of the book, WHOSE, in the following manner:

WHO	WHOSE
Some Kind of Life	The Making of a Care Culture
Moms and Machines	Super I/Poor Me
On the Move	Eucharistic Energy
Heroes	I Count, You Count
Dad's World	Tale of Two Sons
What's Going on Out There	Being Different
What Goes Down Comes Up	Mini-Resurrection

Other combinations are possible. But the above arrangement can assist you in developing your own match-up of chapters.